Greek Orthodox Church in Santorini.

For my husband, Jim,
and my four wonderful children:
Angela, Connie, Victoria and James

With love.

My Big, Fat, Greek Cookbook

Edited by Connie Pitenis

ABOUT THE AUTHOR

Elaine Pitenis grew up in Cambridge, Massachusetts, and did her graduate work in Microbiology and Immunology at Harvard University. She worked in the fields of Microbiology and Cancer Research before marrying and having four beautiful children. The family moved to Greece in 1999 and lived in Athens before relocating to Daytona Beach, FL and opening her Greek Cooking School.

While in Greece, Elaine learned cooking techniques from several acclaimed Greek Chefs from Corinth, Kastoria, and the islands of Samos, Santorini, and Salamina. Chef Elaine began teaching Greek Cooking in 2004 at The Casements in Ormond Beach, FL and has used the acquired techniques from Greece in addition to her prior knowledge of the culinary arts through her mother Connie Spinos, who was an exceptional Home Economics teacher in Cambridge, Massachusetts before she retired.

My Big, Fat, Greek Cookbook elicits a fusion of both "old world," traditional cooking techniques as well as Chef Elaine's own flavorful and innovative methods to offer her readers a unique cookbook containing delicious, heart-healthy Grecian recipes.

My Big, Fat, Greek Cooking Class at The Casements in Ormond Beach.

Register for classes at www.mybigfatgreekcookingclass.com

TABLE OF CONTENTS

FUN WITH PHYLLO

Temple of Olympian Zeus, Athens, Greece.

Phyllo is sometimes pronounced fī -lō or fee-lō. Either way, phyllo dough is a wonderful pastry dough that is used to make dozens of great appetizers, main courses, and desserts. You can find phyllo dough in the frozen food section of the grocery store, usually next to the frozen pie shells. Store phyllo dough in the freezer. The day before you want to use it, take it out of the freezer, place it in the refrigerator, and allow it to thaw overnight. On the day you plan to use it, take it out of the refrigerator and leave it out on the counter for at least two hours to bring to room temperature.

When you are ready to use the phyllo with the other ingredients, keep a damp, clean towel next to you on your work surface. Once the phyllo is opened, it is susceptible to dry out quickly, so the damp towel is necessary to prevent it from drying out. Remove phyllo from packaging and lay out the phyllo flat to make sure the product is not gummy or damaged.

When not working with the phyllo, cover the phyllo in the plastic wrap it comes in, and re-wrap the phyllo. Then take the damp towel and cover the plastic wrap, which will protect the phyllo for at least a half hour.

For some recipes, line the bottom of the baking sheet with aluminum foil and coat lightly with vegetable spray.

When making the phyllo triangles, use the flag-folding technique.

APPETIZERS AND MEZETHES

Santorini and the island of Thira in the distance.

CRAB MEAT WRAPPED IN PHYLLO

Prep: 30 min • Cook: 30 min • Makes 30 triangles

Ingredients

1 small white onion, finely chopped
1 tablespoon sweet unsalted butter
16 oz. cream cheese, softened
4 oz. feta cheese
12 oz. cottage cheese
2 eggs
12 oz. fresh crab meat (picked over to remove cartilage)
1 lb. phyllo dough, room temperature
2 sticks sweet unsalted butter

For the Filling

Preheat oven to 350°F degrees. Sauté onion in unsalted butter. Allow to cool. Combine cheeses in a large bowl. Add eggs, until just combined. Add sautéed onions and fold in crabmeat. Warm 2 sticks unsalted butter until melted.

For the Phyllo Dough

Remove phyllo dough from box and lay flat. Cut phyllo dough into 3 long equal strips. Cover with plastic wrap and a damp towel to prevent drying. Take 2 long phyllo strips and overlap 1 inch to form one long strip. Using a pastry brush, dab butter where they overlap, then lightly dab the entire length of phyllo dough strip.

To Assemble

Place 1 heaping teaspoon crabmeat/cheese filling and fold into triangles using the flag folding technique (p. 9). Butter tops of triangles and place on a buttered baking tray.

Repeat with remaining crab mixture and bake for 25-30 minutes or until golden brown.

SAGANAKI (FLAMING GREEK CHEESE)

Prep: 5 min • Cook: 6 min • Serves 2 to 4

Ingredients

½ lb. imported cheese: Kasseri, Kefalograviera, or Haloumi (available at Greek or Middle Eastern specialty markets)
1 tablespoon olive oil
1 egg, beaten plus 2 tablespoons water
1 cup all-purpose flour
Juice of 1 lemon
1.5 oz. Metaxa Brandy
Greek white bread or French bread (lightly toasted)

To Make Cheese

Coat cast iron skillet with olive oil place over medium heat. Slice the kasseri cheese into ¼ inch thick round slices and dip in egg wash, then coat in flour. Tap off excess flour. Place floured kasseri in hot pan and cook 3 minutes on each side until bubbly and slightly soft. Remove from heat.

Add ~0.25 oz. of the Metaxa brandy to the pan and carefully flame cheese (using a long match or long lighter).

Opa! Squeeze lemon juice over flaming cheese to extinguish flames.

Repeat with remaining slices of cheese. Serve with crusty bread and a good Greek red wine.

KALAMARI (SQUID)

Prep: 15 min • Cook: 5 min • Serves 1 to 3

Ingredients

2 lbs. fresh squid, cleaned and sliced in small rings
2 cups all-purpose flour
½ cup corn meal
3 tablespoons corn starch
1 teaspoon salt
1 teaspoon black pepper
Sunflower or vegetable oil for frying
Lemon wedges
Marinara sauce (optional)

To Make Kalamari

Pat dry squid rings (kalamari) with paper towels. In a deep fryer, heat oil to medium-high heat (375°F).

In a large bowl, combine flour, corn meal, cornstarch, salt and pepper. Coat kalamari in the seasoned flour/corn meal mixture. Shake off excess and carefully place in heated oil in small batches. Deep-fry each batch 3-4 minutes or until golden brown. Carefully remove with slotted spoon and place on plate with paper towels to remove excess oil.

Squeeze with lemon wedges and serve with marinara sauce, if desired.

HUMMUS

Prep: 5 min • Serves 2 to 4

Ingredients
10 oz. chick peas
¼ cup lemon juice
¼ cup extra virgin olive oil
3 or 4 garlic cloves, minced
¼ cup tahini (optional)

To Make Hummus
Combine all ingredients in blender or food processor until smooth.

Serve with pita bread or fresh vegetables.

Variations
Add 3 oz. of roasted red peppers or sun-dried tomatoes to blender. Pulse then serve.

LOUKANIKO MEATBALLS

Prep: 15 min • Cook: 30 min • Makes 30 meatballs

Ingredients

1 lb. ground pork
½ lb. lean ground beef
¼ cup 2% milk
1 tablespoon parsley, chopped
½ cup parmesan cheese, grated
1 tablespoon orange peel, grated
Salt and pepper, to taste
Crushed red pepper, to taste

To Make Meatballs

Combine all ingredients and mix well. Roll into small 1-inch balls. Place on a baking pan lined with foil and bake at 350°F for 30 minutes or until well done.

Gently shake baking pan half way through to unstick if necessary. Allow to cool, and then transfer to a platter.

Serve with lemon wedges as a garnish, if desired.

TZATZIKI (CUCUMBER YOGURT SAUCE)

Prep: 10 min • Serves 4 to 6

Ingredients

32 oz. container plain low-fat Greek yogurt
1 peeled, deseeded cucumber or English cucumber, grated
3 or 4 garlic cloves, minced
Dill (optional)

To Make Tzatziki

Grate cucumber and squeeze out liquid using cheesecloth. Discard cucumber juice. Mix together yogurt with grated cucumber in large bowl. Add minced garlic.

Mix and serve with pita bread. Great when served with souvlaki (p. 46-49).

TARAMOSALATA (RED CAVIAR DIP)

Prep: 5 min • Serves 4 to 6

Ingredients
10 oz. jar tarama caviar (available at
Greek or Middle Eastern specialty markets)
1 loaf (1 lb.) soft mountain bread
Bowl of water
¾ cup extra virgin olive oil
1 medium white onion, finely grated
¾ cup lemon juice
Kalamata olives, lemon slices, or parsley for garnish

To Make Taramosalata
Slice the loaf of bread in half. Set aside. Moisten the bread in bowl of water and squeeze to remove most of the excess liquid. In a food processor, place moistened bread and half the jar of tarama caviar, and pulse until soft. Add the onion and pulse again. Drizzle the olive oil and lemon juice, alternately, and continue to blend until the mixture becomes smooth. Pour into a serving bowl and garnish with olives, lemon slices, or parsley. Serve with pita bread.

Tip: The remaining jar of tarama caviar can be frozen for up to 3 months.

MELITZANOSALATA (EGGPLANT DIP)

Prep: 10 min • Cook: 50-60 min • Serves 3 to 4

Ingredients
1 large eggplant
1 red onion, chopped
½ cup olive oil
¼ cup lemon juice
2 garlic cloves, minced
Salt and pepper, to taste
Kalamata olives and lemon slices for garnish

To Make Melitzanosalata
Cut eggplant lengthwise in half and place face down on oiled baking tray. Bake 50-60 minutes in 350°F oven until soft. (For quicker baking time, the eggplant can also be sliced into ½ inch slices, coated with olive oil, and baked for 30 minutes at 350°F).

Allow to cool. Using a spoon, scoop out eggplant flesh and blend in a food processor with onion, garlic, and lemon juice, pulsing while adding the olive oil gradually.

Chill in the refrigerator for at least 1 hour, allowing the all the flavors to mingle. Serve with pita bread.

DOLMADES (STUFFED GRAPE LEAVES)

Prep: 20 min • Cook: 40 min • Makes 50

Ingredients

16 oz. jar grape leaves, or 50 fresh leaves
from a grape vine
2 lbs. lean ground beef
1 large yellow onion, finely chopped
8 oz. tomato sauce
2 tablespoons parsley, finely chopped
2 teaspoons fresh mint, finely chopped
¾ cup long grain rice, uncooked
2 cups chicken broth
½ cup lemon juice

Egg-lemon Sauce

2 eggs
¼ cup lemon juice

To Make Egg-Lemon Sauce

Beat 2 eggs along with ¼-cup lemon juice
in large bowl. After dolmades are cooked
and slightly cooled, temper hot broth from
cooking pot and gradually whip together
broth with the egg-lemon mixture. Pour
mixture over pot of dolmades and cook
another 5 minutes on low heat. Serve
warm.

To Make Dolmades

Remove grapes leaves from jar, clip off the
stems and blanch in boiling water 10 minutes
and drain. Combine ground beef, onion,
tomato sauce, parsley, mint and rice. Mix well.
To assemble, shape 1-2 tablespoons beef/rice
mixture into 2-3 inch "cigar shapes" and place
on each leaf vein side up. Fold in the sides
covering the meat and roll upward. To prevent
dolmades from burning, arrange a few grape
leaves flat on the bottom of a large 8-quart
cooking pot and place the stuffed grape leaves
in rows over the leaves. Continue until the
entire meat filling has been used.

Pour enough chicken broth and lemon juice
to cover the dolmades. Place a heatproof plate
over the dolmades to keep them in place during
cooking and cover pot with lid. Simmer for
about 30-35 minutes or until rice is cooked.

12

GRILLED OCTOPUS

Ingredients
1 large octopus (about 3 pounds)

Marinade
½ cup olive oil
1/3   cup lemon juice
1 teaspoon Greek oregano
½ teaspoon black pepper
2 garlic cloves, minced

To Make Grilled Octopus
Wash and clean the exterior of the octopus by peeling any outer skin.

To tenderize the octopus, place the octopus in a large pot and cover, simmering over low heat with no liquid in the pot, for about an hour, until the octopus is tender and bright pink. The octopus will exude its own juices while in the cookpot. Remove octopus from the pot and drain. Allow to cool.

Cut the octopus into smaller pieces by its tentacles. Combine marinade ingredients in a bowl and allow the octopus to marinate 4-5 hours, or overnight. Grill octopus over medium heat, brushing it occasionally with the marinade, until it is slightly charred and crisp. Serve immediately.

SKORDALIA (GARLIC DIP)

Prep: 30 min • Serves 4 to 6

Ingredients
6-8 garlic cloves, minced
4 russet potatoes, peeled and boiled until
soft, cooled
½ cup fresh lemon juice
½ cup olive oil
Salt and pepper, to taste

To Make Skordalia
Place garlic, potatoes, and lemon juice in a blender or food processor. Blend until smooth.
Drizzle olive oil into feeding tube and pulse until desired consistency. Makes about 2 cups.

Great when served with baked fish (p. 45) or beet salad (p. 18). Garnish with paprika, if
desired.

SALADS

Speedboat passing by Santorini Harbor.

GREEK SALAD

Prep: 10 min • Serves 4 to 6

Ingredients

16 oz. bagged salad, or washed and cut
romaine lettuce
1 green pepper, sliced
1 tomato, sliced
1 cucumber, peeled and sliced
½ cup parsley, chopped
4 oz. feta cheese, crumbled
Kalamata olives

Dressing

½ cup extra virgin olive oil
½ cup red wine vinegar
¼ cup brine from Kalamata olives
½ teaspoon Greek oregano
Salt and pepper, to taste

To Assemble

Combine salad ingredients and combine
dressing ingredients. Add desired amount of
dressing to salad just before serving.

Serve with warm pita bread.

VILLAGE GREEK SALAD

Prep: 10 min • Serves 3 to 4

Ingredients
2 green peppers, sliced
2 tomatoes, sliced
2 cucumbers, peeled and sliced
1 red onion, sliced
4 oz. feta cheese, crumbled
Kalamata olives

Dressing
¼ cup extra virgin olive oil
¼ cup red wine vinegar
¼ cup brine from Kalamata olives
½ teaspoon Greek oregano
Salt and pepper, to taste

To Assemble
Combine salad ingredients and combine dressing ingredients. Add desired amount of dressing to salad just before serving.

Serve with warm pita bread.

BEET SALAD

Prep: 10 min • Cook: 1 hour • Serves 3 to 4

Ingredients

1 large bunch fresh beets, leaves and roots removed
1 red onion, sliced
2 garlic cloves, minced
1/3   cup olive oil
3 tablespoons red wine vinegar
½ teaspoon Greek oregano
Salt and pepper, to taste

To Assemble

Scrub beets until clean and wrap tightly in foil. Roast in the oven at 350˚F or outside on the grill on medium heat for 1 hour, turning once. Remove when knife can be inserted easily. Let cool.

Remove foil and peel off skins from beets. Slice beets and arrange on a plate with sliced red onions. Mix oil, vinegar, and seasonings, and pour over the beets and onions. Add garlic and serve hot or cold.

Traditionally, skordalia (p. 14) is served with the beets instead of oil and vinegar.

SOUPS

A fishing boat in Greece.

FASOLATHA (BEAN SOUP)

Prep: 1 hour • Cook: 2-3 hours • Serves 8 to 10

Ingredients

1 lb. dried Great Northern Beans, or Navy Beans
½ cup olive oil
1 large white onion, chopped
3 carrots, chopped
3 celery stalks, chopped
½ cup parsley, chopped
8 oz. tomato sauce
½ teaspoon Greek oregano
Salt and pepper, to taste

To Make Fasolatha

Soak beans in a pot of water overnight. Drain. Place beans in an 8-quart pot and add enough water to cover the beans. Bring to a boil over medium-high heat, uncovered for 10 minutes, and drain again.

Add enough water to cover the beans, plus an additional 2 cups water, and add the chopped vegetables, tomato sauce, parsley, olive oil, salt, pepper, and oregano.

Simmer uncovered for 1-2 hours, stirring occasionally, or until beans are tender.

Tip: Add extra water as it boils down.

FAKI (LENTIL SOUP)

Prep: 30 min • Cook: 1 hour • Serves 8 to 10

Ingredients
1 lb. dried lentils
1 large white onion, chopped
3 celery stalks, chopped
3 carrots, chopped
1 garlic clove, minced
8 oz. tomato sauce
½ teaspoon Greek oregano
Salt and pepper, to taste
Red wine vinegar (optional)

To Make Faki
Place lentils in an 8-quart pot and add enough water to cover. Bring to a boil over high heat, uncovered for 10 minutes. Drain.

Add enough water to cover the lentils, plus 2 cups of water, and add the chopped vegetables, tomato sauce, olive oil, and spices.

Simmer uncovered for 1 hour, stirring occasionally, or until vegetables are tender. Add vinegar to taste, if desired.

AVGOLEMONO (GREEK LEMON CHICKEN SOUP)

Prep: 10 min • Cook: 20-25 min • Serves 6

Ingredients
8 cups chicken stock
1 cup short grain rice, or orzo pasta
1 cup cooked, shredded chicken (optional)
2 eggs
1/2 cup fresh lemon juice
Salt and pepper, to taste

To Make Avgolemono
In a stockpot, bring the chicken stock to a low boil and add the rice (or orzo). Simmer until cooked, and then stir in the shredded chicken just to heat through. Season to taste. Remove from the heat and let cool 10 minutes.

In a medium bowl, beat the eggs together with the lemon juice. Carefully temper eggs by slowly drizzling some of the hot broth from the soup into the egg-lemon mixture, whisking constantly so as not to curdle the eggs. Slowly pour the whole mixture back into the stockpot, whisking constantly. A thick consistency is desired. Add fresh ground pepper and serve with lemon wedges, if desired.

Tip: Add more lemon juice for additional lemon flavor.

PSAROSOUPA (FISH SOUP)

Prep: 30 min • Cook: 1 hour • Serves 6

Ingredients
3 lbs. fresh white fish, cleaned and deboned
½ cup short grain rice
3 carrots, chopped
4 celery stalks, chopped
½ cup parsley, finely chopped
1/3 cup olive oil
3 eggs
8 cups water
½ cup lemon juice
Salt and pepper, to taste

To Make Psarosoupa
Cut fish into 3-inch pieces and set aside. Bring water to a boil in a large pot and add vegetables, oil, salt and pepper. Cook for about 30 minutes, or until vegetables are tender.

Add rice. Simmer for 10 minutes. Add fish and continue to cook another 10 minutes until fish and rice is cooked.

In a medium bowl, beat the eggs together with the lemon juice. Carefully temper eggs by slowly drizzling some of the hot broth from the soup into the egg-lemon mixture, whisking constantly so as not to curdle the eggs. Slowly pour the whole mixture back into the stockpot, whisking constantly. A thick consistency is desired.

YOUVARELAKIA (MEATBALL SOUP)

Prep: 15 min • Cook: 45 minutes • Serves 6 to 8

Ingredients
2 lbs. extra-lean ground beef
1 large white onion, chopped
½ cup uncooked short grain white rice
6 cups chicken broth
4 tablespoons fresh parsley, chopped
5 eggs
½ cup fresh lemon juice
Salt and pepper, to taste

To Make Youvarelakia
In a large mixing bowl, add ground beef, chopped onions, parsley, rice, and 2 eggs. Mix well. Form the mixture into 1-inch meatballs. Drop carefully into a large pot of simmering chicken broth, and simmer for 30 minutes or until rice and beef are cooked. Allow to cool.

In a medium bowl, beat 3 eggs together with the lemon juice. Carefully temper eggs by slowly drizzling some of the hot broth from the soup into the egg-lemon mixture, whisking constantly so as not to curdle the eggs. Slowly pour the whole mixture back into the stockpot, whisking constantly. A thick consistency is desired.

SIDE DISHES

Monastery of Saint John the Theologian on the island of Patmos.

RICE PILAF

Prep: 10 min • Cook: 20 min • Serves 6

Ingredients

½ cup thin vermicelli noodles
¼ stick sweet unsalted butter
2 cups converted rice
4 cups chicken broth

To Make Rice Pilaf

In a 2-quart saucepan, sauté vermicelli noodles in butter on medium heat for about 10 minutes, or until golden brown. Add rice and quickly sauté. Add chicken broth and stir.

Reduce heat, cover with lid, and simmer 20 minutes.

Great with a dollop of Greek yogurt.

HORTA (BOILED GREENS)

Prep: 10 min • Cook: 10 min • Serves 2

Ingredients
2 lbs. greens of your choice (dandelions, Swiss chard, etc.)
¼ cup extra virgin olive oil
¼ lemon juice

To Make Horta
Wash several times in warm water. Drain. Cut off stem ends and discard. Chop into 3-inch pieces and add to a large pot. Add 1 cup of water and bring to a boil. Cook 10 minutes on medium heat until tender, stirring occasionally. Drain and transfer to a serving platter.

Add olive oil and lemon juice and serve.

SPANAKORIZZO (SPINACH AND RICE)

Prep: 10 min • Cook: 30 min • Serves 6

Ingredients

1 lb. pre-washed baby spinach
¼ cup extra virgin olive oil
1 medium white onion, chopped
8 oz. tomato sauce
1 cup converted rice
½ teaspoon salt
½ teaspoon pepper
2 cups water, or chicken broth

To Make Spanakorizzo

Sauté onion in oil for about 5 minutes. Add tomato sauce and water and bring to a boil.

Add spinach and cook for 5 more minutes. Add the rice, salt and pepper.

Cover and cook for 20 minutes or until rice is tender.

GREEK-STYLE STRING BEANS

Prep: 10 min • Cook: 40 min • Serves 2 to 4

Ingredients

2 lbs. fresh string beans, washed and ends cut off

1 medium white onion, chopped

¼ cup olive oil

1 cup tomato sauce

1 cup water

½ cup parsley, chopped

Salt and pepper, to taste

To Make String Beans

In large saucepan, cook onion in olive oil until translucent, about 7 minutes.

Add string beans, tomato sauce, water, parsley, salt and pepper. Stir. Cover pan and cook over medium heat for 30 minutes.

Serve warm with fresh bread.

GREEK–STYLE GREEN PEAS

Prep: 5 min • Cook: 20 min • Serves 2 to 4

Ingredients

2 cups green peas, fresh, frozen or canned
1 cup tomato sauce
1 medium onion, chopped
3 tablespoons olive oil
1 teaspoon dill
Salt and pepper, to taste

To Make Green Peas

In large sauté pan, cook onion in olive oil until translucent, about 7 minutes.

Add peas, tomato sauce, salt and pepper. Stir. Cook over medium heat for 10 minutes. Sprinkle with dill and serve.

GREEK-STYLE BAKED POTATOES

Prep: 10 min • Cook: 1 hour • Serves 6 to 8

Ingredients

10 russet potatoes, peeled and cut into quarters, length-wise

½ cup olive oil

5 tablespoons sweet unsalted butter, melted

½ cup fresh lemon juice

1 cup vegetarian broth

1 teaspoon ground pepper

½ teaspoon salt

1 teaspoon Greek oregano

1 teaspoon paprika

To Make Baked Potatoes

Place cut potato slices in large baking pan and add oil, lemon juice, butter, and vegetable broth. Sprinkle with salt, pepper, oregano, and paprika.

Bake at 350°F for 1 hour, or until potatoes are golden brown, slightly crispy at the edges.

Tip: Chicken broth can be used instead for non-vegetarian alternative.

HOMEMADE PITA BREAD

Prep: 30 min • Rise: 2 hours • Cook: 8 min • Makes 10-12

Ingredients
1 pkg. active dry yeast
3 ½ - 4 cups all-purpose flour
1 tablespoon sugar
1 teaspoon salt
1 tablespoon extra virgin olive oil
1 ¼ cups warm water (about 110° to 115°F)

To Prepare Yeast
In a large bowl, dissolve yeast in 1 cup of warm water, add sugar and stir. Cover bowl with plastic wrap. Let stand 10 minutes in a warm place until bubbles form on surface.

To Prepare Dough
In a separate bowl, sift 3 cups of flour and salt. Form a well in center and pour yeast mixture and any remaining water. Mix by hand and add additional flour if needed. Turn out onto a floured surface and knead for about 10-15 minutes, until smooth and no longer sticky.

Coat dough in oil and place in an oiled bowl. Set aside in a warm place free of drafts for 1 ½ to 2 hours, or until doubled in size. Knead for 1 minute and then divide into balls about 2 ½ inches in diameter. Roll balls into circles on a lightly floured surface with rolling pin or flatten into circles with the palm of your hand.

To Bake
Preheat oven to 475°F and bake each pita bread (3 or 4 at a time) for about 4 minutes until the breads puff up. Carefully turn pitas over and bake for 4 minutes until both sides are lightly brown. Remove to wire racks to cool. Let rise on oiled baking sheets for about 20 minutes in a warm place.

MAIN COURSES

Santorini from the bow of the cruise ship.

SPANAKOPITA (SPINACH AND FETA CHEESE TRIANGLES)

Prep: 45 min • Cook: 30 min • Makes 35-45 triangles

Ingredients
1 pint low-fat cottage cheese
2 eggs
1 cup low-fat mozzarella cheese, grated
½ lb. feta cheese, crumbled
1 lb. pre-washed baby spinach
1 small white onion, chopped
2 sticks and 2 tablespoons sweet unsalted butter, melted
1 lb. phyllo dough, room temperature

To Prepare Filling
In a large bowl, combine first 4 ingredients and mix well.

In sauté pan, combine spinach leaves, onion and 2 tablespoons butter. Cook for 10 minutes and let cool. Add to bowl and mix well.

To Prepare Phyllo
Remove phyllo dough from box and lay flat. Cut phyllo dough into 3 long strips and cover with plastic wrap and a damp towel to prevent drying. Take 2 long phyllo strips and overlap 1 inch to form one long strip. Butter edge where they overlap. Lightly dab entire length with melted butter using a pastry brush.

To Assemble
Place 1 heaping teaspoon of spinach/cheese filling and fold into triangles using the flag folding technique (p. 2). Butter tops of triangles and place on buttered baking tray. Repeat with remaining mixture. Bake in preheated 350°F oven for 30 minutes or until golden brown.

CLASSIC SPANAKOPITA (SPINACH AND FETA CHEESE PIE)

Prep: 25 min • Cook: 40 min • Serves 12

Ingredients

1 pint low-fat cottage cheese
½ lb. firm low-fat tofu (optional)
2 eggs
1 cup low-fat mozzarella cheese, grated
½ lb. feta cheese, crumbled
16 oz. baby spinach leaves, prewashed
1 medium white onion, chopped
2 sticks + 2 tablespoons sweet unsalted
butter
1 lb. phyllo dough, room temperature

To Make Filling

Combine first 5 ingredients and mix well. In sauté pan, combine spinach leaves, onion and 2 tablespoons butter. Sauté until spinach is wilted. Add to bowl when cooled and mix.

To Assemble

Melt 2 sticks of butter in a saucepan. Remove phyllo dough from box and lay flat. Butter the bottom and sides of a large 13" x 9" x 3" baking dish. Lay one sheet of phyllo dough on the bottom of the baking pan and brush lightly with melted butter using a pastry brush. Layer another sheet of phyllo dough and repeat process until 10-15 sheets are completed.

Pour spinach and cheese filling into the baking pan and spread evenly. Continue layering 10-15 more phyllo dough sheets and melted butter. With a sharp knife, score desired sized pieces and bake in a preheated 350°F oven for 40 minutes or until golden brown.

SPANAKOPITA ROLL-UPS

Prep: 45 min • Cook: 30 min • Makes: 30 to 40

Ingredients

1 pint low-fat cottage cheese
2 eggs
1 cup low-fat mozzarella cheese, grated
½ lb. feta cheese, crumbled
16 oz. baby spinach leaves, prewashed
1 medium white onion, chopped
2 sticks + 2 tablespoons sweet unsalted butter
1 lb. phyllo dough, room temperature

To Make Filling

Combine first 4 ingredients and mix well. In sauté pan, combine spinach leaves, onion and 2 tablespoons butter. Sauté until spinach is wilted. Add to bowl when cooled and mix.

To Assemble

Remove phyllo dough from box and lay flat. Cover phyllo with plastic wrap and damp towel to prevent drying. Take one sheet of phyllo dough and lightly dab with melted butter.

Fold in half and add a large dollop of spanakopita filling onto the lower half of the sheet. Fold sides on top of filling and roll-up. Seal with melted butter and place on a foil lined baking tray, sprayed with vegetable spray. Brush top of roll-up with melted butter.

Repeat with remaining mixture and phyllo, and bake in a preheated 350°F oven for 30 minutes or until golden brown.

ROASTED LEG OF LAMB

Prep: 10 min • Cook: 8 to 10 hours • Serves 6 to 8

Ingredients
8 lbs. fresh or frozen leg of lamb (New Zealand or Australian baby lamb)
1 head garlic, cleaned and slivered
3 tablespoons olive oil
3 tablespoons soy sauce

To Prepare
Defrost frozen leg of lamb and carve away all the excess fat. Using a sharp knife, stab a little hole and insert a garlic sliver. Continue inserting garlic slivers throughout the lamb leg (25-30 slivers). Rub lamb leg with olive oil and soy sauce.

To Roast Lamb
Place lamb leg in roasting pan and bake on high heat (500°F) for 20 minutes uncovered. Reduce heat to 225°F and cover with a tightly sealed foil tent and cook slowly for 8-10 hours until juicy and tender.

Great with Greek-style baked potatoes (p. 31) and a glass of red wine!

MOUSSAKA

Prep: 1 hr 30 min • Cook: 40 minutes • Serves 10 to 12

Ingredients

Meat Sauce Layer
3 lbs. lean ground beef
1 large white onion
¼ cup olive oil
12 oz. tomato sauce
1 teaspoon Greek oregano
2 teaspoons ground cinnamon
1 cup water
Salt and pepper, to taste

Vegetable Layer
3 large eggplants
6 zucchini
6 russet potatoes
½ cup olive oil
Salt and pepper
1½ cups Pecorino Romano cheese, grated
1 cup low-fat Ricotta cheese

Béchamel Sauce
¼ cup sweet unsalted butter
1 cup all-purpose flour
5 cups 2% milk
4 eggs
1½ cups Pecorino Romano cheese, grated
1 cup low-fat Ricotta cheese

To Prepare Meat Sauce Layer

Heat olive oil in a sauté pan over medium-high heat. Add onion and cook until translucent. Add the meat and cook until no longer pink. Add tomato sauce, seasonings, and 1 cup of water. Simmer uncovered 1 hour, stirring occasionally. Set aside to cool.

To Prepare Vegetables

Trim ends from eggplant and cut into 3/8 inch thick round slices. Sprinkle salt on both sides of each slice and let sit on paper towels for 30 minutes. Trim ends from zucchini and cut lengthwise into 3/8 inch thick slices and set aside.

Brush eggplant and zucchini slices lightly with olive oil and place on a hot grill. Cook until tender with nice grill marks on both sides. Set aside until ready to assemble. (Vegetables can be oven baked or grilled).

Peel the potatoes and cut into ½- inch slices. Brush both sides lightly with olive oil and place on foil lined baking tray. Sprinkle with salt and pepper. Bake 350°F for 20 minutes covered with foil. Uncover for 15 more minutes or until golden brown and tender.

To Make Béchamel Sauce

In a large saucepan, whisk together butter and flour and cook over medium heat for 4-5 minutes. Slowly add milk and whisk constantly with a wire whisk, until the sauce begins to thicken. Allow the sauce to cool for 10 minutes. Whisk in ricotta cheese and 1-cup Pecorino Romano Cheese, setting aside ½ cup of grated cheese for topping. Whisk in eggs, and set aside.

To Assemble

Preheat oven to 375°F. Using a large, deep pan (11 x 14 and 4" deep), spray bottom and sides with non-stick cooking spray. Arrange 1 layer of baked potato slices over bottom of pan, overlapping if necessary. Arrange zucchini slices over potato, followed by a layer of eggplant slices. Top eggplant with meat sauce and carefully pour béchamel over all. Sprinkle the top with the remaining Pecorino Romano Cheese. Bake uncovered for 40 minutes or until golden brown. Remove from oven and let stand for 20 minutes before serving.

SOUZOUKAKIA (SPICED MEATBALLS)

Prep: 30 min • Cook: 45 min • Serves 8 to 10

Ingredients

Sauce
28 oz. tomato sauce
2 cups water
¼ cup olive oil
½ teaspoon sugar
½ teaspoon Greek oregano

Meat Rolls
1 cup Italian style bread crumbs
2 lbs. lean ground beef
2 eggs
¾ cup milk
½ teaspoon cinnamon
1 garlic clove, minced
1 teaspoon cumin
½ cup parsley, chopped
Salt and pepper, to taste

To Prepare

In a large bowl, combine meat roll ingredients. Wet hands and shape meat into ovals about 3 inches long. Place side by side in baking pan and bake in a preheated 400°F oven for 15 minutes.

Separate if meat rolls are stuck together. Lower heat to 350°F and bake an additional 15 minutes.

While the souzoukakia are baking, place sauce ingredients in a large saucepan. Bring to a boil, lower heat and simmer until thickened.

Add baked souzoukakia to the saucepan and cook in the sauce for 20 more minutes.

Serve on a bed of rice.

LITHRINI STIS SKARA (GRILLED RED SNAPPER)

Prep: 5 min • Cook: 20 min • Serves 2 to 4

Ingredients
2 fresh red snappers, cleaned and scaled
¾ cup olive oil
½ cup fresh lemon juice
2 teaspoons Greek oregano
Salt and pepper, to taste

To Make Lithrini Stis Skara
Coat fish with olive oil and grill slowly on medium-high heat, about 10 minutes on each side. Mix olive oil, lemon juice, oregano, salt, and pepper in bowl and pour over grilled red snapper. Serve warm.

PAPOUTSAKIA (STUFFED EGGPLANTS)

Prep: 1 hour • Cook: 45 minutes • Serves 6

Ingredients

3 large eggplants
2 lbs. lean ground beef
2 garlic cloves, minced
1 large white onion, finely chopped
½ cup fresh parsley, chopped
32 oz. tomato sauce
¼ cup olive oil
1 cup grated kefalotyri cheese (or grated
parmesan cheese)
Salt and pepper, to taste

Béchamel Sauce

½ cup all-purpose flour
3 tablespoons sweet unsalted butter
2 cups 2% milk, room temperature
2 eggs
1 cup grated kefalotyri cheese (or grated
parmesan cheese)

To Prepare Eggplant

Trim off stems from eggplants and cut in half, lengthwise. Brush with olive oil and place face down on a foil-lined baking tray and bake at 350°F for 45 minutes, or until soft. Allow to cool. Flip eggplants over. With a small spoon, press down gently on the pulp leaving space for the filling.

To Make Filling

In large sauté pan, cook the onions in 2 tablespoons of olive oil on medium heat until onions are translucent. Add garlic and ground beef. Sauté thoroughly until beef is no longer pink. Stir in tomato sauce, parsley, salt and pepper, and reduce heat. Simmer covered for 20 minutes. Remove from heat and set aside.

To Make Béchamel Sauce

In a medium saucepan, whisk together butter and flour and cook over medium heat for 4-5 minutes. Slowly add milk and whisk constantly with a wire whisk, until the sauce begins to thicken. Allow the sauce to cool for 10 minutes. Add grated cheese, whisk in eggs, and set aside.

To Assemble

Place each eggplant face up on a foil lined baking tray. Sprinkle some of the cheese to cover the bottom of the well in each eggplant, then spoon in the meat filling to the top of the side rims. Spoon over the béchamel sauce, then sprinkle the remaining grated cheese over the top of each eggplant.

Bake at 350°F for 30 minutes or until the cheese is browned.

Remove the eggplants from the pan and serve warm.

CHICKEN OREGANO

Prep: 10 min • Cook: 35 min • Serves 4

Ingredients

2 lbs. chicken thighs
2 tablespoons Greek oregano
½ cup parsley, chopped
2 tablespoons sweet unsalted butter, melted
3 tablespoons lemon juice
2 tablespoons olive oil
Salt and pepper, to taste

To Make Chicken Oregano

Remove skin from chicken. In a bowl, combine lemon juice, olive oil, oregano, salt and pepper. Rub seasoning onto both sides of chicken.

Place chicken in a lightly greased ovenproof glass baking pan and pour melted butter over chicken. Bake in a preheated 400°F oven for 15 minutes. Turn chicken once, and reduce heat to 350°F. Bake an additional 20 minutes, or until done, basting once with pan juices.

Sprinkle with chopped parsley and serve.

BAKED FISH

Prep: 10 min • Cook: 30 min • Serves 6

Ingredients

3 lb. haddock or cod, cleaned and deboned
¼ cup olive oil
2 tablespoons sweet unsalted butter, melted
½ cup parsley, chopped
1 cup Italian style bread crumbs
½ teaspoon Greek oregano
Lemon wedges
Salt and pepper, to taste

To Make Fish

In a bowl, combine salt, pepper, oregano, parsley and breadcrumbs. Moisten fish by dipping in water. Coat both sides with seasoned breadcrumbs and place in a 9 x 13 inch greased baking dish lined with foil. Drizzle fish with oil and melted butter.

Bake in a preheated 375°F oven for 20 minutes or until fish is golden brown. Baste fish occasionally with pan juices.

Serve with lemon wedges and skordalia (p. 14).

CHICKEN SOUVLAKI

Prep: 15 min • Marinate: 4 hours • Cook: 20 min • Serves 6

Ingredients

3 lbs. boneless, skinless, chicken breast, cut into 1" cubes

Marinade

1 cup extra virgin olive oil
¾ cup lemon juice
1 garlic clove, minced
1 teaspoon salt
1 teaspoon pepper
2 teaspoons Greek oregano

To Prepare

Combine marinade ingredients and set aside. Thread chicken onto skewers. Place skewered meat in plastic food container and pour marinade inside. Cover. Marinate in refrigerator 4 hours, turning meat occasionally.

To Grill

Place skewered meat on hot grill, turning often. Grill until chicken is no longer pink (internal temperature reaches 160°F).

Serve with warm pita bread (p. 32) and tzaziki (p. 9).

LAMB SOUVLAKI

Prep: 15 min • Marinate: 4 hours • Cook: 20 min • Serves 6

Ingredients
3 lbs. lamb shanks, cut into 1-inch cubes

Marinade
1 cup extra virgin olive oil
¾ cup lemon juice
1 garlic clove, minced
1 teaspoon salt
1 teaspoon pepper
2 teaspoons Greek oregano

To Prepare
Combine marinade ingredients and set aside. Thread lamb onto skewers. Place skewered meat in plastic food container and pour marinade inside. Cover. Marinate in refrigerator 4 hours, turning meat occasionally.

To Grill
Place skewered meat on hot grill, turning often. Grill lamb until internal temperature reaches 155°F. Remove from grill and let stand.

To Cook in Oven
Place skewers on a rack of a broiler pan and place them about 6 inches from broiler heat. Turn occasionally and baste with marinade. Broil until internal temperature reaches 155°F.

PORK SOUVLAKI

Prep: 15 min • Marinate: 4 hours • Cook: 20 min • Serves 6

Ingredients

3 lbs. pork tenderloin, cut into 1-inch cubes

Marinade

1 cup extra virgin olive oil
¾ cup lemon juice
1 garlic clove, minced
1 teaspoon salt
1 teaspoon pepper
2 teaspoons Greek oregano

To Prepare

Combine marinade ingredients and set aside. Thread pork onto skewers. Place skewered meat in plastic food container and pour marinade inside. Cover. Marinate in refrigerator 4 hours, turning meat occasionally.

To Grill

Place skewered meat on hot grill, turning often. Grill pork until internal temperature reaches 150°F. Remove from grill and let stand.

To Cook in Oven

Place skewers on a rack of a broiler pan and place them about 6 inches from broiler heat. Turn occasionally and baste with marinade. Broil until internal temperature reaches 150°F.

BEEF SOUVLAKI

Prep: 15 min • Marinate: 4 hours • Cook: 20 min • Serves 6

Ingredients
3 lbs. beef tenderloin, cut into 1-inch cubes

Marinade
1 cup extra virgin olive oil
¾ cup lemon juice
1 garlic clove, minced
1 teaspoon salt
1 teaspoon pepper
2 teaspoons Greek oregano

To Prepare
Combine marinade ingredients and set aside. Thread beef onto skewers. Place skewered meat in plastic food container and pour marinade inside. Cover. Marinate in refrigerator 4 hours, turning meat occasionally.

To Grill
Place skewered meat on hot grill, turning often. Grill beef until internal temperature reaches 160°F. Remove from grill and let stand.

To Cook in Oven
Place skewers on a rack of a broiler pan and place them about 6 inches from broiler heat. Turn occasionally and baste with marinade. Broil until internal temperature reaches 160°F.

BEEFTEKI (BEEF PATTIES)

Prep: 30 min • Cook: 15 min • Makes: 10-12

Ingredients

½ cup Italian style bread crumbs
¼ cup olive oil
1 lb. lean ground beef
½ lb. ground pork
1 egg
1 tablespoon Greek oregano
1 large onion, finely chopped
1 teaspoon thyme (optional)
2 garlic cloves, chopped
3 tablespoons parsley, chopped
¼ cup milk
Salt and pepper, to taste

To Prepare

Sauté onions and garlic in sauté pan containing 1 tablespoon olive oil over medium heat until translucent. Set aside to cool. Combine the ground beef with the ground pork in a large bowl and add the olive oil, milk, egg, sautéed onion and garlic, bread crumbs, parsley, oregano, thyme, salt, and pepper.
Mix until all ingredients are completely combined. Shape the beeftekia into medium sized patties.

To Grill

Oil grill and barbecue patties approximately 5-6 minutes on each side on medium-high heeat.
Serve with marinara sauce.

BEEF WELLINGTON WRAPPED IN PHYLLO

Prep: 30 min • Cook: 40 min • Serves 5

Ingredients

5 filet mignons, 1 ¼ inch thick, 4-5 ounces each

25 white mushrooms, cleaned and coarsely chopped

1 shallot, minced

1 garlic clove, minced

½ cup + 2 tablespoons. sweet unsalted butter, melted

1 tablespoon olive oil

Salt and pepper, to taste

25 sheets of phyllo dough, cut 6" x 6"

Worcestershire sauce (optional)

To Make Mushroom Duxelles

Sauté shallot and garlic until golden brown in 1 tablespoon butter and olive oil. Add mushrooms and cook for several minutes until all moisture has completely evaporated. This can be prepared in advance.

To Make Beef Wellington

Pan-sear filets in a hot skillet, approximately 3 minutes on each side. Set filets aside on plate with paper towels to absorb juices and let cool.

Layer 5 sheets of phyllo dough, dabbing each layer with melted butter. Put 1 filet on layered phyllo dough.

Drizzle ½-teaspoon Worcestershire sauce over filet. Top with 3 tablespoons mushroom duxelles. Fold in sides of phyllo dough and wrap like a present, making sure that filet is completely covered. Seal seams with melted butter. Repeat with remaining filets. Place all on a baking tray with parchment paper, seam side down. Brush each filet with melted butter and bake in a preheated 450°F oven for approximately 7-8 minutes or until golden brown.

PASTITSO

Prep: 2 hours • Cook: 40 minutes • Serves 10 to 12

Ingredients
Meat Sauce Layer
3 lbs. lean ground beef
1 large white onion, diced
12 oz. tomato sauce
1 cup water
½ teaspoon pepper
1 teaspoon Greek oregano
½ teaspoon allspice
2 teaspoons cinnamon

Pasta
2 lbs. pasta (Mostaccioli, Ziti, or Ditalini),
cooked until tender
½ cups Pecorino Romano, grated

Béchamel Sauce
¼ cup sweet unsalted butter
1 cup all-purpose flour
5 cups 2% milk
4 eggs
1½ cups Pecorino Romano cheese, grated

To Make Meat Sauce Layer
Heat olive oil in a sauté pan over medium-high heat. Add onion and cook until translucent. Add the meat and cook until no longer pink. Add tomato sauce, seasonings, and 1 cup of water. Simmer uncovered 1 hour, stirring occasionally. Set aside to cool.

To Make Béchamel Sauce
In a large saucepan, whisk together butter and flour and cook over medium heat for 4-5 minutes. Slowly add milk and whisk constantly with a wire whisk, until the sauce begins to thicken. Allow the sauce to cool for 10 minutes. Whisk in 1-cup Pecorino Romano Cheese, setting aside ½ cup of grated cheese for topping. Whisk in eggs, and set aside.

To Assemble

Preheat oven to 350°F. Spray a 10 x 14 baking pan with vegetable oil. Add half of the cooked pasta to the pan. Pour 2 cups of the béchamel to coat pasta. Add meat sauce and cover evenly. Cover with remaining pasta and spread remaining béchamel sauce over the top. Sprinkle with remaining grated cheese. Bake 40 minutes or until golden brown.

CHICKEN ATHENIAN

Prep: 4 hours • Cook: 45 min • Serves 4

Ingredients
4 boneless skinless chicken breasts
2 cups tzaziki (p. 16)
¼ cup olive oil
Salt and pepper, to taste
Lemon wedges (optional)

To Make Chicken Athenian
Marinade the chicken in 1 cup of tzaziki for 4 hours, or overnight. In a large skillet, heat olive oil over medium heat. Cook chicken until golden brown and chicken is no longer pink (160°F internal temperature).

Serve on a bed of rice with remaining tzaziki and lemon wedges.

MANESTRA YOUVETSI (BAKED LAMB WITH ORZO)

Prep: 10 min • Cook: 2 hours • Serves 4 to 6

Ingredients
3 lbs. lamb shoulder or leg of lamb
1 medium white onion, halved
4 garlic cloves, whole
16 oz. whole peeled tomatoes
2 cups water
¼ cup sweet unsalted butter
2 cups orzo (rice shaped pasta)
3 cups chicken broth
½ cup grated parmesan cheese
Salt and pepper, to taste

To Make Manestra Youvetsi

Trim fat from the lamb and score it about 1 inch apart. Place the lamb in a "youvetsi" (clay pot), or a large baking pan. Add the onion, garlic, tomatoes, butter, salt, pepper and 2 cups water. Cover and bake in a preheated 400°F oven for 1 ½ hours or until meat is tender. Transfer meat onto a serving platter and keep warm.

In the same baking pan, add the orzo and broth. Stir. Loosely cover pan with aluminum foil and bake until the orzo is cooked and has absorbed all of the liquid. Stir occasionally and add additional water, if necessary.

When orzo is cooked, remove onion and garlic. Cut lamb into large serving pieces and arrange over orzo. Sprinkle with parmesan cheese and serve warm.

YEMISTA (STUFFED PEPPERS AND TOMATOES)

Prep: 30 min • Cook: 1 hr 30 min • Serves 6 to 8

Ingredients

2 lbs. lean ground beef
4 large bell peppers, red or green
4 large ripe tomatoes
1 large white onion, chopped
2 cups chicken broth
1 cup long-grain rice
¾ cup fresh parsley, chopped
¼ cup olive oil
Salt and pepper, to taste

To Prepare Tomatoes and Peppers

Wash all vegetables well and cut a cap off the top of each tomato. Scoop out tomato pulp and put in a bowl. Set tomatoes and caps aside. Cut a cap off the top of each bell pepper, scoop out seeds, and rinse well. Stab peppers and tomatoes several times with sharp knife. Set peppers, tomatoes, and caps aside.

To Prepare Rice

Place rice in medium saucepan and add 1 cup water. Cook 10 minutes until partly cooked, and most of the water has been absorbed. Allow to cool.

To Prepare Stuffing

Chop all the pulp that was scooped out from the tomatoes and place in a large bowl. Add cooled par-cooked rice, ground beef, onion, parsley, salt, pepper, and olive oil. Mix well. Fill the tomatoes and peppers with the meat stuffing to within 1/2 inch of the top. Place caps on top of tomatoes and peppers.

To Assemble

Brush bottom of 9 X 13 baking pan with olive oil. Place the stuffed tomatoes and peppers in the baking pan, placing them upright so they fit snugly in the pan. Add chicken broth to the pan. Cover with foil. Preheat oven to 450˚F. Bake until the liquid starts to boil, and then reduce heat to 350˚F. Cook for one hour. Remove cover and continue to cook until rice is thoroughly cooked.

PAITHAKIA (GRILLED LAMB CHOPS)

Prep: 5 min • Cook: 6 min • Serves 2

Ingredients
5 lamb chops
½ cup olive oil
½ cup fresh lemon juice
2 teaspoons Greek oregano
Salt and pepper, to taste

To Make Paithakia
Grill lamb chops on medium-hot grill for 3 minutes on each side. Mix olive oil, lemon juice, oregano, salt, pepper in bowl and pour over grilled lamb chops, and serve.

YIAYIA ELENI'S THANKSGIVING STUFFING

Prep: 30 min • Cook: 40 min • Serves 6 to 8

Ingredients

2 lbs. lean ground beef
1 large white onion, chopped
3 carrots, peeled and chopped
3 celery stalks, chopped
1 small green pepper, finely chopped
1 cup long grain rice, uncooked
2 apples, peeled and coarsely chopped
1 cup dark raisins
1 cup toasted chestnuts, coarsely chopped (optional)
2 cups chicken broth

To Make Stuffing

In large stockpot, sauté ground beef until fully cooked. Add all chopped ingredients, rice, and chicken stock. Stir well. Cover and cook about 30-40 minutes. Stir in raisins and chestnuts and cook an additional 5 minutes. Serve with turkey and cranberry sauce.

VEGETARIAN MAIN COURSES

Caryatids on the Erechtheion at the Acropolis.

VEGETARIAN MOUSSAKA

Prep: 2 hours • Cook: 1 hour • Serves 10 to 12

Ingredients
Homemade Tomato Sauce
1 large white onion, chopped
2 teaspoons garlic, minced
2 teaspoons ground cinnamon
29 oz. crushed tomatoes
1 cup vegetable broth
2 tablespoons Greek oregano
2 teaspoons fresh mint leaves, minced
2 teaspoons balsamic vinegar
1 tablespoon brown sugar
¼ teaspoon salt
¼ teaspoon freshly ground black pepper
2 teaspoons olive oil

Vegetables
2 large eggplants
5 medium zucchini
6 russet potatoes
½ cup olive oil

Béchamel Sauce
½ cup all-purpose flour
4 tablespoons sweet unsalted butter
5 cups 2% milk
1 cup Parmesan cheese, grated
1 cup low-fat ricotta cheese
2 eggs, lightly beaten
Salt and pepper, to taste

To Prepare Tomato Sauce
Heat olive oil in a large pot over medium-high heat. Add in onions and garlic. Cook and stir until onions are softened, about 3 minutes. Stir in cinnamon and cook 1 more minute. Add crushed tomatoes, broth, oregano, mint, balsamic vinegar, sugar, salt and pepper. Mix well. Cover with a splatter screen and simmer gently over medium heat for 2 hours, stirring occasionally.

To Prepare Vegetables
Trim ends from eggplant and cut into 3/8 -inch thick round slices. Sprinkle salt on both sides of each slice and let sit on paper towels for 30 minutes. Trim ends from zucchini and cut lengthwise into 3/8 -inch thick slices and set aside.

Brush eggplant and zucchini slices lightly with olive oil and place on a hot grill. Cook until tender with nice grill marks on both sides. Set aside until ready to assemble. (Vegetables can be oven baked or grilled).

Peel the potatoes and cut into ½- inch slices. Brush both sides lightly with olive oil and place on foil lined baking tray. Sprinkle with salt and pepper. Bake 350°F for 20 minutes covered with foil. Uncover for 15 more minutes or until golden brown and tender.

To Make Béchamel Sauce

In a large saucepan, whisk together butter and flour and cook over medium heat for 4-5 minutes. Slowly add milk and whisk constantly with a wire whisk, until the sauce begins to thicken. Allow the sauce to cool for 10 minutes. Whisk in ricotta cheese and Parmesan cheese, setting aside ½ cup Parmesan cheese for topping. Whisk in eggs, and set aside.

To Assemble

Preheat oven to 375°F. Using a large, deep pan (11 x 14 and 4" deep), spray bottom and sides with non-stick cooking spray. Arrange 1 layer of baked potato slices over bottom of pan, overlapping if necessary. Arrange zucchini slices over potato, followed by a layer of eggplant slices. Top eggplant with thick tomato sauce and carefully pour béchamel over all. Sprinkle the top with the remaining Parmesan cheese. Bake uncovered for 40 minutes or until golden brown. Remove from oven and let stand for 20 minutes before serving.

VILLAGE SPANAKOPITA

Prep: 1 hour • Cook: 45 min • Serves 12

Ingredients
Filling
1 pint low-fat cottage cheese
2 eggs
1 cup low-fat mozzarella cheese, grated
½ lb. feta cheese, crumbled
16 oz. baby spinach leaves, prewashed
1 white onion, chopped
2 sticks + 2 tablespoons sweet unsalted butter

Homemade Phyllo Pastry
4 cups all-purpose flour
½ teaspoon salt
1 cup hot water
½ cup olive oil

To Make Filling
Combine first 4 ingredients and mix well. In sauté pan, combine spinach leaves, onion, and 2 tablespoons butter. Sauté until spinach leaves are wilted. Add to bowl when cooled and mix. Set aside.

To Make Dough
Using a food processor, add flour, salt, and olive oil. While pulsing, stream hot water through feeding tube until a soft dough forms. Remove from food processor and allow to rest 10 minutes. Using rolling pin, roll out dough until very thin on a floured surface. Spoon enough melted butter to cover entire surface, and spread evenly using your hand. Starting at one side, roll into a log then turn log to form a spiral. Allow to rest 10 minutes. Cut dough into two halves. Using rolling pin, roll out each portion of dough until very thin with slightly stretchy consistency.

To Assemble

Butter the bottom and sides of a large baking pan. Place one thin dough layer on the bottom of the pan, overlapping the sides by a half inch. Add filling and spread evenly. Place the remaining dough layer on top, crimping edges to seal. Top with melted butter and bake at 350˚F for 15 minutes. Poke holes with sharp knife wherever air bubbles have formed. Bake another 30 minutes or until golden brown. Removed from oven and push 10 butter knives under the bottom layer to prevent moisture from softening the bottom crust. Allow to cool 20 minutes. Serve warm.

GIGANTES (GIANT LIMA BEANS)

Prep: 30 min • Cook: 2 hours • Serves 6

Ingredients

1 lb. dried giant lima beans
1 cup parsley, chopped
1 large green pepper, chopped
1 large red pepper, chopped
2 medium onions, sliced
16 oz. petite chopped tomatoes
1 cup tomato sauce
2 tablespoons Greek oregano
2/3 cup olive oil
½ teaspoon crushed red pepper
6 garlic cloves, chopped
1 cup vegetable broth
Salt and pepper, to taste

To Make Gigantes

Place beans in a large pot. Fill the pot with enough water to cover the beans. Bring to a boil, simmer for 15 minutes. Drain.

Fill pot again with enough water to cover the beans and 3 more cups of water. Simmer uncovered for 30-40 minutes or until tender. Drain.

In a large mixing bowl, add cooked lima beans with remaining ingredients and stir together. Pour mixture onto a baking tray and bake uncovered for 30-45 minutes at 350°F.

Serve warm.

DESSERTS

Temple of Olympian Zeus & Arch of Hadrian Athens, Greece.

HALVA

Prep: 15 min • Cook: 20 min • Serves 8 to 10

Ingredients
2 cups Cream of Wheat (farina)

1 stick sweet unsalted butter

Syrup
1 ¾ cups sugar

3 cups water

1 ½ teaspoons cinnamon

To Make Syrup
In medium saucepan, boil the 3 syrup ingredients for 10 minutes.

To Make Halva
In a large saucepan, sauté the butter and the farina, stirring constantly for 10-15 minutes on medium heat until golden brown.

Remove from heat. Slowly and carefully, pour boiling syrup onto farina mixture and mix well. Cover and let sit for 5 minutes until syrup is absorbed. Spoon hot halva into a serving mold that has been sprayed with vegetable spray and press halva into place. Allow to cool in the mold for at least 2 hours. Invert onto a serving platter and serve.

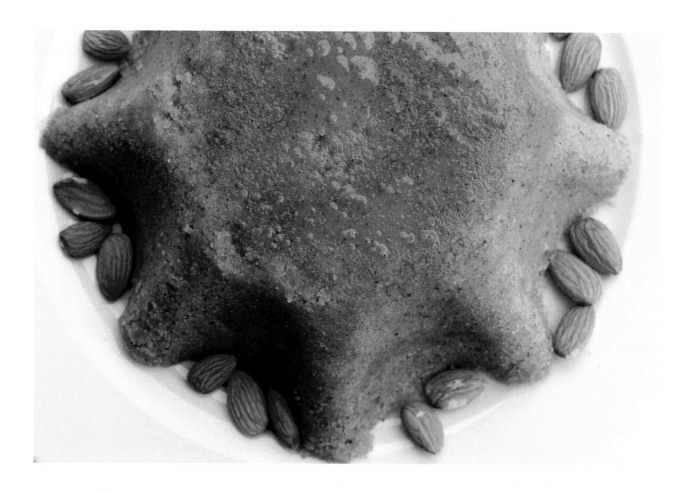

LOUKOUMADES (HONEY BALLS)

Prep: 2 hours • Cook: 25 min • Makes: 60

Ingredients
Dough
1 cup buttermilk, scalded
¼ cup sweet unsalted butter
1 tablespoon sugar
½ teaspoon salt
1 pkg. yeast
1 egg
3 cups all-purpose flour
Vegetable oil, for frying
Cinnamon, for sprinkling

Syrup
2 cups sugar
1 cup water
½ cup honey

To Make Syrup
Bring syrup ingredients to a boil and simmer for 10 minutes. Cool.

To Make Dough
Combine first four ingredients and cool to lukewarm by adding ½ cup water. Add yeast and mix well. Blend in egg. Add flour and mix until batter is well blended. Cover with plastic wrap and let rise until it has doubled in volume (about 2 hours).

To Fry
Using two teaspoons, dip spoons into hot oil, then take a heaping teaspoon of batter and carefully drop batter in hot oil in deep fryer. Fry for 2-3 minutes on each side. Drain on paper towels. Serve with honey-syrup and sprinkle with cinnamon.

FINIKIA (HONEY DIPPED COOKIES)

Prep: 20 min • Cook: 25 min • Makes: 24

Ingredients

Cookie Dough

1/3 cup sugar
¾ cup vegetable oil
½ cup fresh orange juice
1 egg
3 ½ cups all-purpose flour
1 teaspoon orange zest
1 teaspoon cinnamon
1 teaspoon baking powder
1 teaspoon baking soda

Syrup

1 cup sugar
½ cup water
½ cup honey
1 cup fresh orange juice
1 cinnamon stick
1 teaspoon orange zest

Topping

1 cup walnuts, crushed
½ teaspoon cinnamon
1 tablespoon sugar
Honey, for drizzling

To Make Finikia

Cream together sugar and oil for 2 minutes with electric mixer. Add orange juice, egg, and orange zest, and mix well. Sift together flour, cinnamon, baking soda and baking powder. Stir dry ingredients into mixture. Knead well to form a ball, adding more flour if necessary. Pinch off small pieces of dough and form into oval shapes. Place on a baking sheet lined with parchment paper. Bake at 350°F for 20-25 minutes or until golden brown. Allow to cool.

In a medium saucepan, combine syrup ingredients and boil for 10 minutes then simmer for another 5 minutes. Dip several finikia in syrup allowing syrup to be absorbed (2 minutes). Using a slotted spoon, remove finikia and drip on wire rack.

Combine crushed walnuts, cinnamon and sugar. Drizzle honey on top of each finikia and sprinkle tops with walnut topping. Serve in baking papers.

KOURAMBIETHES (POWDERED SUGAR BUTTER COOKIES)

Prep: 40 min • Cook: 20 min • Makes: 48

Ingredients

1 lb. sweet unsalted butter
¾ cup sifted confectioners' sugar
1 egg yolk
1.5 oz. cognac
4 to 4 ½ cups all-purpose flour, sifted
1 teaspoon baking powder
1/3 cup blanched almonds, toasted and finely chopped
Confectioners' sugar for sprinkling

To Make Dough

Let butter soften in a large bowl at room temperature. Sift sugar into butter gradually and cream thoroughly using electric hand mixer. Add egg yolk and cognac and mix well. Add finely chopped almonds to butter mixture. Sift flour and baking powder together. Gradually work enough flour to butter mixture to make a soft dough that is pliable and easy to handle. Knead lightly, wrap in wax paper, and chill for 30 minutes.

To Bake Kourambiethes

Form balls about 1 ½ inches in diameter and shape into crescents. Arrange on ungreased cookie sheets, about 1 inch apart.

Bake in a preheated 325°F oven for 20 minutes, or until the cookies are a pale sand color. Remove from oven.

Sprinkle with confectioners' sugar while still hot. When cooled, sprinkle with additional powdered sugar before placing them into baking papers.

KOULOURAKIA (SESAME TWIST BUTTER COOKIES)

Prep: 20 min • Cook: 20 min • Makes: 20 to 25

Ingredients

1 stick sweet unsalted butter
½ cup sugar
1 egg
1 teaspoon vanilla extract
1 ¾ to 2 cups all-purpose flour, sifted
1 teaspoon baking powder
Egg wash (1 egg + 2 tablespoons water)
Sesame seeds

To Make Koulourakia

Sift dry ingredients and set aside. Cream butter, sugar, eggs, and vanilla in a large bowl using an electric hand mixer. Add just enough flour to the bowl to form a ball. Pinch off small pieces of dough and form into a 6-inch log. Twist dough into desired shapes and place on a baking sheet.

Brush egg wash onto each cookie and sprinkle with sesame seeds. Bake in a pre-heated 350°F oven for 20 minutes until golden brown.

BAKLAVA

Prep: 15 min • Cook: 30 min • Makes: 48

Ingredients
1 lb. phyllo dough, room temperature
½ lb. sweet unsalted butter, melted

Filling
2 lbs. walnuts, chopped
½ cup sugar
2 teaspoons cinnamon

Syrup
2 ½ cups sugar
½ cups honey
1 ½ cups water
2 teaspoons cinnamon
1 tablespoon lemon juice

To Make Syrup
Bring syrup ingredients to a boil and simmer 10 minutes. Cool.

To Assemble
In a large bowl, add sugar, cinnamon and chopped walnuts and mix. Set aside. Remove phyllo dough from box. Butter large baking tray and place one sheet of phyllo dough. Dab lightly with melted butter using a pastry brush. Repeat with 15 layers of phyllo dough. Spread half of the walnut filling on the top layer and repeat adding phyllo dough/melted butter for 8 layers. Spread remaining walnut filling and repeat with the remaining layers of phyllo and melted butter. Spread a thin layer of melted butter on top. Cover evenly. Using a sharp knife carefully cut into serving pieces before baking. Bake at 350°F for about 30 minutes or until golden brown. Cool 1 hour before adding syrup. Allow syrup to soak 2 minutes, and then carefully pour off excess. Cut through each piece with sharp knife and serve in silver baking papers.

GALAKTOBOUREKO (GREEK CUSTARD WITH PHYLLO)

Prep: 30 min • Cook: 45 min • Serves 15

Ingredients
Custard Filling
1 cup Cream of Wheat (farina)

6 eggs

1 cup sugar

6 cups milk

Zest from one lemon

1 lb. phyllo dough

½ lb. sweet unsalted butter, melted

Syrup
2 cups sugar

1 cup water

2 tablespoons lemon juice

To Make Syrup
In saucepan, boil the syrup ingredients for 10 minutes. Cool.

To Make Galaktoboureko
Before placing large saucepan over heat, place the farina and eggs in the saucepan and whisk to blend. Add milk, sugar, and lemon zest. Then cook over medium heat, stirring continuously until it thickens, 10-15 minutes. Set aside to prepare the baking dish. Brush 10 x 14 deep-dish baking pan with melted butter and layer it with 20 individually buttered phyllo sheets, allowing phyllo sheets to overlap the edges.

Carefully pour hot custard over the bottom phyllo sheets and fold phyllo edges over custard. Top with 20 more individually buttered phyllo sheets, tucking in sides on each layer for a neat finish.

With a sharp knife, score the top phyllo sheets into 3-inch squares. Bake in a preheated 350°F oven for 40 minutes or until golden brown. Remove and cool. Spoon warm syrup over the cooled pastry. Cut through each piece with sharp knife and serve.

BAKLAVA ROLL UPS

Prep: 10 min • Cook: 10 min • Makes: 100

Ingredients
1 lb. phyllo dough
½ lb. sweet unsalted butter, melted
2 lbs. walnuts, chopped
½ cup sugar
2 tablespoons cinnamon

Syrup
2 ½ cups sugar
½ cups honey
1 ½ cups water
2 teaspoons cinnamon
1 tablespoon lemon juice

To Make Syrup
Bring syrup ingredients to a boil and simmer 10 minutes. Cool.

To Make Walnut Mixture
Combine chopped walnuts, cinnamon and sugar in a bowl. Set aside.

To Make Baklava
Remove phyllo dough from box, lay flat and cover with a clean damp towel to keep from drying. Place one sheet of phyllo on a flat surface and brush lightly with melted butter. Repeat with two more sheets of phyllo. Spoon 3 tablespoons of the walnut mixture over the bottom edge of the phyllo rectangle. Carefully rollup the phyllo, covering the walnuts, and forming a log roll shape. Brush roll lightly with melted butter. Place seam-side down in cookie sheet pan that has been sprayed with vegetable spray. Repeat with remaining phyllo and walnut filling, laying each rollup next to the other so they are about an inch apart. Cut log rolls into 1 ½-inch pieces. Bake in 350˚F oven for 10 minutes or until golden brown. Allow to cool 10 minutes, and then spoon cooled syrup over rollups. Serve in baking papers.

BAKLAVA TRUFFLES

Prep: 2 hr 30 min • Makes: 30

Ingredients

8 oz. semi-sweet or bittersweet chocolate
(high quality 62% cacao)
1/2 cup heavy whipping cream
1 teaspoon vanilla extract (optional)

Truffle Coatings

Unsweetened cocoa powder
8 servings of Baklava, crumbled

To Make Ganache

In a small, heavy saucepan bring the heavy whipping cream to a simmer (stir and scrape down the sides with a spatula every few minutes). Place the chocolate morsels in a large bowl and carefully pour the scalding cream over the chocolate. Add the vanilla and let stand for 10 minutes. Using a rubber spatula, stir until smooth and allow to cool. Place in the refrigerator for a minimum of two hours.

To Assemble

Using a spoon, scoop out 1 inch balls of the ganache. Roll each in cocoa powder, and then roll in crushed baklava. Serve in small baking papers, or place in the refrigerator until needed.

Baklava Truffles can be frozen in a sealed container for up to 3 months.

RIZOGALO (RICE PUDDING)

Prep: 5 min • Cook: 45 min • Serves 4

Ingredients

4 cups 2% milk
1/3 cup short grain white rice
½ cup granulated sugar
1 teaspoon vanilla extract
Ground cinnamon, for sprinkling

To Make Rizogalo

Place the milk in a saucepan and add rice and sugar. Stir frequently with wooden spoon over medium heat for 40-45 minutes, until the rice is tender and has a thick consistency.

Mix in the vanilla and pour into 4 individual bowls. Sprinkle each bowl with cinnamon before serving.

Serve warm or cold.

KATAIFI (SHREDED PHYLLO DOUGH)

Prep: 15 min • Cook: 35 min • Makes: 10 to 12

Ingredients

1 lb. kataifi dough*
1 lb. chopped walnuts
½ cup sugar
1 teaspoon cinnamon
½ lb. sweet unsalted butter, melted

Syrup

½ cup honey
2 cups sugar
2 cups water
2 tablespoons lemon juice

*Dough can be found in the frozen section at Greek or Middle Eastern market.

To Make Syrup

Boil syrup ingredients for 10 minutes. Allow to cool.

To Make Kataifi

In a large bowl, mix the walnuts, sugar, and cinnamon. Brush the bottom of a 9" x 13" baking pan with melted butter. Open the kataifi dough, tear off a 6" x 3" section, and lay flat. Keep remainder of pastry dough covered with plastic wrap and a damp cloth. Drizzle 2 teaspoons of melted butter over kataifi dough. Add 2 tablespoons of walnut mixture at one end of the pastry and roll up loosely.

Place on baking pan and sprinkle with melted butter. Repeat with remaining kataifi dough. Sprinkle a few drops of cold water on top of each kataifi. Bake at 350°F for 35 minutes or until golden brown. Let cool for 10 minutes. Slowly pour warm syrup over the kataifi letting it soak in.

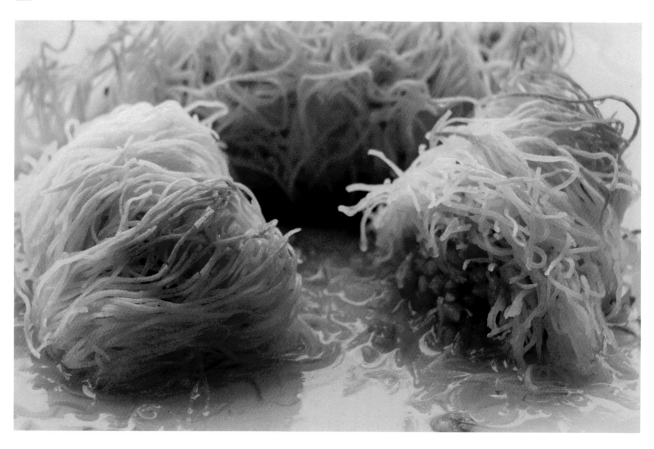

BEVERAGES

Santorini Beachside Restaurant.

COLD COFFEE FRAPPÉ

Prep: 5 min • Serves 1

Ingredients

1 cup cold water
Ice cubes
Instant coffee (NesCafe)
Milk (optional)
Sugar (optional)
Whipped cream (optional)

To Make Frappé

In a jar or shaker with a tight-fitting lid, add 4 tablespoons of cold water, 1 teaspoon of instant coffee, and sugar to taste. Close lid tightly and shake for 20 seconds, until foamy.

Pour into a tall glass, add 8 ounces of water, ice cubes, milk and sugar to taste, and stir.

Serve with a dollop of whipped cream, cinnamon, or ground chocolate!

GREEK COFFEE

Prep: 10 min • Serves 2

Ingredients
Greek coffee
Sugar
Cold water
1 briki (pronounced BREE-kee)
2 Demitasse cups

To Make Coffee
Pour cold water into a briki, two-thirds full. Add 2 teaspoons of Greek coffee, and 1 teaspoon of sugar to the briki. Stir with a spoon. Over medium heat, stir the coffee until it dissolves and allow it to create foam as it boils. The foam (kaimaki) will start to rise in the briki just as it begins to boil. When the foam rises to the top of the briki (it can rise very quickly once it starts to boil), remove from heat. Pour some foam in each of the two demitasse cups then return briki to the heat and allow foam to form again. Pour remainder into cups. Allow coffee to settle at least 5 minutes before sipping.

Do not drink the bottom half of the Greek coffee as the layer of "mud" at the bottom of the cup is not intended for drinking.

LEMONOUZO

Prep: 5 min • Serves 1

Ingredients
8 oz. pink lemonade
1 oz. Ouzo
¼ cup freshly squeezed lemon juice
Ice cubes

To Make Lemonouzo

Combine ingredients and serve over ice. Opa!

ACKNOWLEDGEMENTS

Agios Nektarios Monastery.

Many thanks to all the great chefs and home cooks who contributed to the manuscript.

Thank you to my wonderful neighbors, JoAnn and Ed Fischer, who ignited my passion for cooking Greek cuisine.

And thanks to The Casements in Ormond Beach, Florida for giving me the opportunity to teach Greek Cuisine to thousands of wonderful students since 2004.

REGISTER FOR CLASSES!

Sign up for classes at
www.mybigfatgreekcookingclass.com

The Casements
25 Riverside Dr
Ormond Beach, FL 32176

PHOTOGRAPHY CREDITS

Agios Nektarios Church in Aegina.

Nikki Ross, Daytona Beach News-Journal
Emily Blackwood, Ormond Beach Observer Newspaper
Chef Elaine Pitenis, The Casements
Ako Stark
Angela Pitenis

INDEX